PASSING WORLDS

PASSING WORLDS

TAHITI IN THE ERA OF CAPTAIN COOK

POEMS

ELIZABETH HOLMES

LOUISIANA STATE UNIVERSITY PRESS   BATON ROUGE

Published by Louisiana State University Press
Copyright © 2018 by Elizabeth Holmes
All rights reserved
Manufactured in the United States of America
LSU Press Paperback Original
First printing

Designer: Barbara Neely Bourgoyne
Typeface: Whitman
Printer and binder: LSI

"Not Recorded: Dorlton and Richmond, Servants," "Not Recorded: Girl," and "Joseph Banks, Botanist and Patron" first appeared in the *Southern Review*. "Babel of Signs" first appeared in *Plume* (plumepoetry.com).

LIBRARY OF CONGRESS CATALOGING-IN-PUBLICATION DATA
Names: Holmes, Elizabeth Ann, 1957– author.
Title: Passing worlds : Tahiti in the era of Captain Cook : poems / Elizabeth Holmes.
Description: Baton Rouge : Louisiana State University Press, [2018]
Identifiers: LCCN 2017056657| ISBN 978-0-8071-6823-3 (pbk. : alk. paper) |
    ISBN 978-0-8071-6824-0 (pdf) | ISBN 978-0-8071-6825-7 (epub)
Classification: LCC PS3558.O3592 A6 2018 | DDC 811/.54—dc23
LC record available at https://lccn.loc.gov/2017056657

The paper in this book meets the guidelines for permanence and durability of the Committee on Production Guidelines for Book Longevity of the Council on Library Resources. ∞

Any culture tells you how to live your one and only life: to wit, as everyone else does.... Time and the peoples it bears issu[e] from the mouth of the cosmos, from the round mouth of eternity, in a wide and parti-colored utterance. In the complex weave of this utterance like fabric, in its infinite domestic interstices, the centuries and continents and classes dwell. Each people knows only its own squares in the weave, its wars and instruments and arts, and also perhaps the starry sky.

—ANNIE DILLARD, "This Is the Life"

CONTENTS

Prophecy 1

The Dolphin
Iron 5
George Robertson's Poem 6
Approach 7
Babel of Signs 8
The Landing 10
Marae 11
Purea, a "Great Woman" 12
Skin 14
Not Recorded: Girl 15
Nails 16
Tupaia, High Priest 17

The Brief Adventure of the French
Points of Interest 21
A Tahitian in Paris 22

The Endeavour, *from England to the South Pacific*
James Douglas, 14th Earl of Morton, President of the Royal Society 25
The Mission 26
James Cook, Captain 28
Provisions 29
Joseph Banks, Botanist and Patron 30
Daniel Solander, Botanist 32
Sydney Parkinson, Artist 34
Not Recorded: Dorlton and Richmond, Servants 35
Sailors 37
Parkinson on Board 40
Richmond and Dorlton: Night 41
Tierra del Fuego 42
Cook: The Nature of Seamen 44

One Look Back
Elizabeth Batts Cook 47

The Endeavour *at Tahiti*
Reef 51
Fa'a, an Old Priest 53
Fa'a, Ambassador 54
Impressions of the Natives of
    King George's Island 55
Parkinson: Morality 57
Parkinson: Dye-Making 58
Incident 59
And Everywhere There Was
    Joseph Banks 62
The Sailors Prepare to Depart 64
Cook: Departure 65
Tupaia Leaving 66

Counterpoint
Truth Is the Daughter of Time 71
In Matavai Bay 72
Incidental 74
Possession 76
The Chief Mourner 78
Counterpoint 80

Afterword 83

ACKNOWLEDGMENTS 87
NOTES 89
SELECTED SOURCES 93

PASSING WORLDS

PROPHECY

Something strange was coming—
huge, with lights on it,
moving across the sea.
Were the beings on it people,
or ancestors, or gods?

Some said it was a floating island
as Tahiti in the beginning floated,
an enormous shark, until a god
fixed its shape and place. Others
remembered the priest Vaita
in our most bitter defeat,
distraught, trance-struck:

The glorious children of Tetumu
will come. Their body is different,
our body is different. We are one
species only from Tetumu.
This land will be taken by them.
The old rules will be destroyed.
They are coming
on a canoe with no outrigger.

The DOLPHIN

AT TAHITI, JUNE–JULY 1767

CAPTAIN SAMUEL WALLIS

IRON

In earth an ore, a rust-red vein
A streak in hematite or blackband ironstone
A taste in the water

Mined, smelted, fired and forced
into cast bars for the blacksmith's anvil
Hammered to hard shape, hard use

On a ship, by the hundreds, bolts, rings,
spikes, hinges, plates, nails, hooks

In the hold, for trade with the natives,
hatchets and knives

In the hands of marines
musket and bayonet, balls, small shot

On Tahiti
none. Until.

GEORGE ROBERTSON'S POEM

Our Seamen now falling doun in the Scurvey Wing fast
(weak and nervous, gums rotten) the Capt and us
spears our fresh stock to the Sick (teeth falling out, legs
stiff and purpled with ulcers, urine green) but it runs Short—
our hay Made in the Streights of Magellan
for our sheep is now near done
but very few peas to keep them upp—the poor hogs
could not walk the Deck without falling—

but fine weather and plenty of Water, no man
restricted from Drink at the Water Casks

This Day we saw a very Great Bird
likeways flying fish and some tropic Birds
gave us all great hopes of Seeing some happey place

(boats repaired ready for landing) a fine ten Oar Cutter
Swivel Stock for Shiping four Musquetoons
we Likeways train up all our Boats Crews to Small Arms
as for the Great Guns we Exercise them frequently

all Earnestly wishing to fall in with some well Inhabited Country
as to Landing and Searching there Countrys
with no fire Arms, no great Dificulty in that

every man wishd to find what he liked most,
some wanted Good Beef, others Sheep or Hogs—
some fowls and oythers Vegetables as the Doctor
tould them for curing the Scurvey

Oythers hearty and well wished for
wild Game, Gold, Silver, Diamonds
Pearls & some for fine young Girls

APPROACH

A land *uneven as a piece of*
crumpled paper precipitous heights
and dark valleys *a beautiful verdure*
even to the tops of the highest peaks

Closing in, they crowded the deck to stare
into unfathomed depths, a heaven
of hues remembered, heard of:
meadow, shamrock, mottled apple,
subtle moss and tender peas, fairy-tale
emerald, Chinese jade, mallard,
peacock, wind-whistled barley,
darkest yew of cemetery lanes

They plunged, they drowned in plush
abundance, earth-born wealth, as they had
not yet *praise God* drowned
in the slippery, bilious shades of the sea

BABEL OF SIGNS

Skirting the coast desperate for fresh food
cutter nosing in for soundings

miles offshore they anchor overnight
wake in thick fog-bank that abruptly lifts:
surrounded: 300 canoes:
a tremendous din of wild yells

      (the first Europeans they had ever seen)

bold young man comes aboard, friendly
steals a hat, marines point muskets

      (he perceives no threat)

moving on, at last a fine bay sheltered
the soundings good here safety at last

      (it is winter solstice, the gods farewelled
      to the dark world of spirits, canoes
      beached, the sea forbidden to all

      but daring a fleet sets out to investigate
      the strange craft that violates *tapu*)

drop anchor, some trading for food
suspicion, air of indistinct hostility

barge and cutter press in toward the river
with empty water casks
a fast canoe rams the cutter
shears off the mizzen boom, warriors
spring up to board, the first Tahitian
ever gun-shot dies

      (they pull him up to stand
      he falls again
      they help him sit but he topples back

      yet not one stranger has touched him
      not with stone or club or spear
      have they given him death)

back off, take time
a bit more edgy trading for pigs and fruit

again the boats seeking fresh water
surf too high to land but thousands
crowd the shore, beckoning

      (it is a gesture of dismissal)

near-naked lush girls start a nasty
chant, thrust hips, sway big breasts,
show genitals to gaping sailors
who gobble up wanton enticement

      (it is pure derision, taunting weak men
      with female power)

red and yellow feathers brought in canoes
handed up to the captain he thinks
it is a gift

      (it is an invitation to war)

THE LANDING

'Oro had surely come among us! His priests
must have conjured this floating island,
its sides lined with his sacred red and yellow.
God of two spheres, did he come in his guise
of rich fertility, or wearing the bloody mask of war?

Strange beings lived on this island, perhaps
ancestors emerged from the dark world below.
Their terrible power! Warriors in canoes attacked,
and then came 'Oro's deafening thunder—
smoke—canoes splintered—trees felled—
many dead on land, and the bay
slick with the blood of the best men.
What had we unleashed?   In scarlet clothes
they came ashore, spoke words of ceremony,
raised a pole with a red cloth, asserting their rule.
We trembled before the cloth, so clearly imbued
with their awful might, and laid before it
plantain boughs in sign of human sacrifice,
and gifts of pigs and fruit. But when they returned
to their island, we carried it off to the temple
to bind its power to our own.

MARAE

open temple, solid mass of coral stones
place of a high chief, descendant of gods
place of the feather-covered god-image
shadow place, overhung with sacred trees

a portal, *jawbones of the gods, biting the spirits*
who passed into the dark underworld

on nearby paths men and women
dropped their garments to the waist
in sign of awe and hurried on

unlucky wanderer killed with a stone
carried to the *marae* trussed to a pole
when the deep drum sounded people
miles around stilled their hands
hushed their children
put out their fires

PUREA, A "GREAT WOMAN"

Peace made with the terrible strangers, I saw
at once how very useful they could be.
These were no ancestors, only men,
though men with vast powers. Many ill,
even their chief small and sickly.
I gave him feasts of pig, I made the girls
massage his painful legs. With the best bark-cloth
I wrapped him into my kinship, with a necklace
of my own hair I bound him. Now, allied
with the strangers' might, I cannot fail
to make my little son the high chief.

The *marae* grows wider and taller, white
coral stone by stone. The high priest Tupaia
has seen to the sacrifice buried at each corner.
There my son shall be invested, priests
wrapping him in the red feather girdle, chanting,
the air tense as hot breath of sky before storm,
chanting as 'Oro nears, drawn by fresh sacrifice.

And we will rule—I and my husband Amo
and shrewd Tupaia—until the boy is grown.

For this I gave up the rich life of the *'arioi*,
lords of ceremony—I the best dancer, I
who led them all, so pleasing 'Oro
that fruit burst from the blossoms of trees,
sows grew heavy with piglets, women
turned to their husbands and conceived.

Once before my belly swelled.
When the pains were over I gave one glance
to the wizened infant and nodded to Amo.
He strangled her at once. Not for us

the shame: to lose the rank of *'arioi*.
Not for me the disgraceful name
whannownow, bearer of children. Yet,
this time, let Amo shout and swear,
I brought the baby to my breast.

I surrendered the honor, wealth, liberty—
for in the moment of birth my body
swelled with a storm-wind, my ears
with a god-voice, and at first sight
of the infant I knew the glorious future:

As we travel my son's lands, all will bow
and offer gifts, and his soft feet
will not touch the earth. His eyes—so beautiful!
deep as the secret heart of an *aute* flower—
will flash from time through time
with sacred lightning.

SKIN

Those of inferior rank
fishermen
dark brown
a light copper colour
swarthy

Superiors who stay in the shade
seldom browner (the women especially)
than the *Brunette which many in Europe*
prefer to the finest red and white

Some in between
mulatto
mustee

The lightest girls
not so fair as our English Ladies
but *infinitely too much so*
for their copper-coloured husbands

NOT RECORDED: GIRL

She was sixteen or twelve or ten, and she bathed
in the river three times a day. Possibly
virgin, probably smoothed her hair
with coconut oil, her legs and buttocks likely
dark with elaborate tattoos. And was she curious
when chosen (ordered?) to lie with a stranger—
old or young but surely stinking,
rippled with muscle from a life at sea or
weak with ulcered skin and rotten teeth?
Surprised? that a face like bark had a body root-
white, hair on the chest (attracted?) a man
frantic for sex, man from an unimaginable (did she
imagine?) land, and what was it like to feel
his breath, his hands, his penis, and when
he was done, go home (relieved? proud? sullied?
weeping?) with a nail—tool of rare unbreakable
iron, sharp to speed the work of men.

Picture her handing it over. She walks
alone to the river, waving off the greedy flies,
and steps in up to her neck. She lays
the back of her head on the water and stares
so deep in the sea of the sky, her body
grows lighter, her feet lift from the sand.
Imagine her, as the water glides
around her and on, imagining herself
gazing down on the island world,
on Mount Orohena where rivers are born,
down on the casuarinas and palms
where parrots flash and hide their colors,
down on the river that parts for a girl, bathing.

NAILS

They used them for carving or drilling
bent some into fishhooks

and planted a few
to see if they'd grow.

TUPAIA, HIGH PRIEST

I took the name Tupaia—beaten—
when I came to Tahiti. Scars still
fresh. Driven from my own Ra'iatea
when Boraboran warriors rampaged,
slaughtered, seized the land
and desecrated 'Oro's sacred place
to our bitter grief and shame.
Tupaia—not despair but resolve:
I will never be beaten again.

On Ra'iatea I grew tall, wrestling
under the palms, diving among coral
and bright fish. Chosen for learning,
for priesthood, I recited history,
proverbs, prayers, the stars
and constellations, lineage
of the highest born, how the universe
came to be. Learned to navigate
vast distances by sun and stars,
the signs of birds, the subtle
currents of wind and water.

So skilled I am acknowledged
a master wayfinder. Yet, until
Ra'iatea is free, a wayfinder
who cannot find his way home.

Now come these strangers
from a land called Peretani.
I think of Vaita's prophecy.
They kill in a moment as many
as a flock of birds, strike farther
than the strongest archer.
When they make peace I advise Purea

to bind them close, so no other chief
dare raise a hand. We begin
a patient courtship.

Filthy men—they never bathe
nor pluck their armpit hair.
Their names are unspeakable,
like the clatter of kicked pebbles.
Though some appear high-born,
their manners are often ill-bred.
Some are entirely stupid.

But their gifts are wondrous:
Large, long-necked chickens. Iron pots,
knives, hatchets. Soft cloth,
seeds of the fruits of Peretani.
A small hairy animal, hardly set down
before it leaps upon a rat, so sudden
we laugh and exclaim.

One day they show us a thing
to look through, into the sky.
The gods are angry, they are
eating the sun, portending war.
I brood on Vaita's words.

Now to our consternation
they are leaving, the boy chief
not yet installed, my homeland
not retaken. Purea weeps. I watch.
The men climb high and rattle down
the sails. They chant to their gods
as they haul up the anchor,
dripping seaweed and sand.
Let us see if they will come again.

THE BRIEF ADVENTURE OF THE FRENCH

who spent ten days on Tahiti in 1768, after the *Dolphin* and before the *Endeavour,* landing on the other side of the island; they were unaware that they were not the first.

———◦———

COMMANDER LOUIS-ANTOINE DE BOUGAINVILLE

POINTS OF INTEREST

The cook sneaked ashore without permission. A crowd stripped off his clothes to see if he was a normal man, then presented a girl and demanded that he have sex with her. He was too terrified.

Tahitians regarded the black slaves as unattractive, but *the whiteness of a European body delighted them.*

Venereal diseases were already rampant thanks to the British, and now the French introduced syphilis. Long after their visit, the afflicted lost hair and nails, their flesh rotted, they died.

Jeanne Baret, disguised as a man to serve as valet to her lover, a distinguished naturalist, was outed by a Tahitian, who recognized her gender at once. Some islanders attempted to carry her off, but an officer drew his sword and stopped them. The next day they stripped her, just to make sure.

They know no other Gods than Love, the naturalist wrote. *Every day is dedicated to it, the entire island is its temple, every woman is its altar, every man its priest.*

Islanders picked the Frenchmen's pockets and hid in a swamp near their camp, reaching into the tents with long hooked sticks to steal things.

The French shot or bayoneted several Tahitians in various altercations.

Unaware of infanticide or human sacrifice, or the frequency of brutal warfare, Bougainville declared Tahiti *the true Utopia.*

A TAHITIAN IN PARIS

A man named Ahutoru sailed back with Bougainville. In Paris he met famous people, enjoyed the nightlife and especially opera, but was mainly interested in women. Seeing a painting of Venus, he pretended to lift her brief drapery and made unmistakable gestures. Many women obliged, but men said he had no taste.

He learned hardly any French and people lost interest; he went to the opera alone. He grew homesick.

Loaded with gifts, from seeds and cattle to jewelry and a coat with gold frogs, he was sent back, but died of smallpox off Mauritius.

Tahiti was the talk of Paris—fertile land of simple, friendly people who never had to work and enjoyed sex without the least restriction or shame. Real-life noble savages.

Although during the long voyage to France Ahutoru had conveyed (in Tahitian) a few sobering facts, the myth had a life of its own. It encouraged revolution.

The
ENDEAVOUR
from England to the South Pacific

AUGUST 1768–APRIL 1769

CAPTAIN JAMES COOK

JAMES DOUGLAS, 14TH EARL OF MORTON, PRESIDENT OF THE ROYAL SOCIETY

Hints offered to the consideration of Captain Cooke, Mr Bankes, Dr Solander, and the other gentlemen who go upon the expedition on board the Endeavour *10 Aug. 1768*

To exercise the utmost patience and forbearance with respect to the Natives of the several Lands where the Ship may touch.

To check the petulance of the Sailors, and restrain the wanton use of Fire Arms.

To have it still in view that sheding the blood of those people is a crime of the highest nature:—They are human creatures, the work of the same omnipotent author, equally under his care with the most polished European; perhaps being less offensive, more entitled to his favour.

They are the natural and, in the strictest sense of the word, the legal possessors of the several Regions they inhabit.

No European Nation has a right to occupy any part of their country, or settle among them without their voluntary consent.

They may naturally and justly attempt to repell intruders, whom they may apprehend are come to disturb them in the quiet possession of their country, whether that apprehension be well or ill founded.

Therefore should they in a hostile manner oppose a landing, and kill some men in the attempt, even this would hardly justify firing among them, 'till every other gentle method had been tried.

THE MISSION

Transit of Venus

Thirteen thousand miles they would sail for this—
to time the passage of Venus across the sun.
Tahiti, newly mapped, the perfect site.
Outposts of science around the globe
would time it too, and touching all these measures
with the sleek wand of trigonometry, men
would make them yield the sun's diameter, and then
the distance earth to sun—the Astronomical Unit—
with which they'd gauge the solar system's span,
the flying planets one through six by gravity
tethered. All that adjudged, they'd reckon next
the universe, entire. A transit of Venus
happens four times in two hundred forty-three years.
The next? Not in the lifetime of anyone living.

Enter Joseph Banks

Young, rich, a capable botanist and naturalist,
returned from exploring the wilds of Newfoundland.
Despises the typical dandy's Grand Tour
(*Every blockhead does that*) and decides
to circle the globe, discovering and naming
living things. Offers, at his own expense,
the naturalists, artists, servants, equipment
to make his adventure an epic success.

Terra Australis

Another, secret mission (front-page rumor
in the *London Gazette*): to sail from Tahiti south
into uncharted waters and claim for George III

the vast Southern Continent. It must exist—
for how could earth steadily rotate, lacking
a counterbalance to the weighty north?
Object of speculation for centuries, surely
teeming with valuable trees and animals, gemstones,
precious metals, inhabited by very different
but hopefully tractable people, potential lynchpin
of a new commercial empire—England must have it,
if only to preempt the greedy French.

JAMES COOK, CAPTAIN

*From a prentice boy in the Coal Trade to a Commander
in the Navy*—such my rise, and rare enough for a Yorkshire
laborer's son, when nearly every officer is gentleman-born.
As if birth could give true authority.

Now, entrusted with His Majesty's bark *Endeavour*,
I must share the captain's cabin with gentlemen,
inexperienced at sea, who add to an overcrowded ship
every book, instrument and tool their science conceivably
may require, as well as four servants (two black)
and two supremely useless dogs. But I'll not quibble.
I am an officer at last, charged with a glorious, arduous
and likely impossible mission: to circumnavigate the globe,
observe the transit of Venus from the South Seas,
and discover, if such exists, the Southern Continent.

To those above my station I show due respect
and hope to earn their genuine regard. *A man
who has not the advantage of Education,* I find
in theirs much to admire. They are sociable,
intelligent men, and wise enough, thus far,
to attempt no interference in the ship's command.

PROVISIONS

4,000 pieces of beef in casks
6,000 pieces of pork
Bread: 21,000 pounds in bags
13,000 in butts
In puncheons, 1,200 gallons of beer
10 carriage guns, 12 swivels

Length of ship: 106 feet
Aboard: 94 men, 2 dogs, a cat,
a pig and piglets, sheep,
1 goat, a flock of poultry

Space between nails that tether
seamen's hammocks: 14 inches

JOSEPH BANKS, BOTANIST AND PATRON

Fourteen and lordly *a great*
Inattention in Him rich boy at Eton
and an immoderate Love of Play
but one warm evening alone
in the gold light of a lane *richly enamelled*
with flowers

for the first time he saw
what flowers are:
under the shimmer of color whose beauty
drew him, near-infinite variety:

a leaf like moist silk, another leather,
saw-toothed, ribbed / blossom's trumpet, hood,
soft spokes / diverse delicate turns of a petal's
fluting / dance of stamen, pistil, pollen, bee—

he would learn botany, learn
the whole natural world.

Rich boy, but only one book—his mother's
tattered *Gerard's Herbal*—and no teacher, Eton
imparting not the thinnest slice of science,
and so

what else became visible? Women.
Poor country women, gypsies, gatherers
of simples, who searched out, dug, picked
and sold to apothecaries their stock in trade.

Their wrinkles and rough hands! Rural accent,
rude grammar. No word of Latin, letter of Greek,
no lady's learning of harpsichord, embroidery,

gavotte, minuet. They made their living
by leaf and flower, berry and root, by knowing
how each in poultice or tea might heal.

Rich boy, yes, but a mind that could listen,
knew when the foreign, the inferior
could teach him. Paid sixpence for each
bit of knowledge, and learned.

DANIEL SOLANDER, BOTANIST

Master Linnaeus, here am I,
your devoted pupil, snugly ensconced
on the ship *Endeavour*. Here, too,
are Joseph Banks, botanist, patron, friend;
his excellent botanical draughtsman,
Parkinson; a landscape artist, Buchan
(skilled but sickly); the astronomer
Charles Green of Greenwich; and under
a sturdy, sensible captain, a rough
and hardy crew who make *such good
philosophers*, they know what specimens
will interest me and fetch them readily
from their nets. Fine companions all!

The heavens grant new birds to our shot,
the sea new fish, and every landfall
genera heretofore unknown. Master,
we carry your gospel to the southern seas,
bestowing names by your brilliant
Systema Naturae ("a masterpiece,"
as you said, "that no one can read too often
or admire too much"). I could compose
an aria, so musical the names. *Medusa
limpidissima, plicata, obliquata!*
Lovely, the liquidity of Latin.

My letters are few, for writing is not
congenial, however friends may scold me
for neglect. It's in the airy spoken word
that I excel, my element the social rhythm—
speak and smile, laugh and listen.

A ship on the open sea provides a fine, fresh
but narrow society. Some days I long

for London: for learned colloquies, rich
collections; kind and clever friends,
both men and women; and night after night,
a glass of port, or two, or three; a generous
cut of beef or tender lamb; potatoes melting
with new-churned butter; and to conclude,
a luscious trifle—custard, sponge cake
laced with sherry, ripest plums
and sweetest cherries, and over all:
cream, whipped to the civilized skies.

SYDNEY PARKINSON, ARTIST

It is the eye that sketches, the hand only
a servant, though one exquisitely attuned
to the eye's intentions. In Mr. Banks' grand
London house, far from the grey stones
of my own Edinburgh, amid rich furnishings,
porcelain, tapestries, I, a plain Quaker,
was engaged for plain things—to draw
with utmost fidelity each natural object gathered
on the wild shores of Newfoundland.
I turned my eye from vanities, and lost myself
in the fine tracings of the wings of a fly.

Yet, not all was plainness, nor rote
transcription of each line and shade
of the creature before me—the fish inert
in alcohol, the dry, stuffed and faded bird.
Because I could, sometimes, by grace, give life—
the fish bright-eyed and gaping, pliant flower
not yet plucked, curlew trembling toward flight—
by Mr. Banks' request, in his employ *I went on board
the ship,* ENDEAVOUR, *then lying in the Galleons
Reach, in the river Thames.*

NOT RECORDED: DORLTON AND RICHMOND, SERVANTS

Endeavour's pitch and yaw likely made him sick—
George Dorlton had sailed maybe just once,
a child from Jamaica, sold in London perhaps
for a lady's page in satin suit and feathered turban,
to carry her fan and smelling salts, her lapdog too,

and set off the whiteness of her skin. The darker
the boy, the higher his price. That part outgrown,
Dorlton hired himself to Banks—hired,
for sometime somebody had set him free.

The greyhounds maybe were in his care.
Pointy-nosed and thin as whips, though he fed them
plenty, twice a day. Gentle dogs, not like the brutes
on Jamaica, Saint Kitts, Martinique—these
hunted nothing bigger than rabbits. If only

they'd learn to use the seat of ease,
where sailors and servants went to crap.
At sea the nightmare let him alone:
On an errand for Banks, alone in the street,

seized from behind, gagged and hustled
to the docks. Months shackled in filth
and darkness, then the short scourged life
of a West Indies slave. Such were the tales
among blacks in London. Many true.

His natural ally on *Endeavour:* the only
other negro, Thomas Richmond, likely also
a freed slave from the islands. A plant collector
trained by a botanist, and by him sent to work for Banks.

They liked each other, or didn't. Surely
at least they shared a few complaints and jokes.
Surely their eyes met and discreetly rolled
when Banks fussed over a peculiar fly,
a bit of seaweed, a squid too small to eat.

Long days at sea, they fetched and carried,
waited perhaps at the captain's table, cleaned
the officers' head of misdirected piss, stoked
the galley stove for the one-handed cook.

Good servants, and Banks a decent master.
Pleased to have black servants—fashionable
in London, their complexion looking so well
against a gentleman's bright livery. Exotic,

did they suggest, to some, a hint of the savage
pleasantly tamed, smoothly brought to heel?
All his long and influential life, Joseph Banks
disliked slavery, on economic grounds.

SAILORS

We came as boys
half-starved, unschooled.
Seamen's sons, at sea
by twelve, or else we'd been
apprentice-slaves to
drapers and cobblers, in
smithies and mills.
An easy choice,
the high-rigged ships,
the hustle and jangle
of foreign ports.
No sort of life
did we have on land.
But all of us fear the sea.

*In heaving the Anchor out of the Boat M^r
Weir Masters mate was carried over board
and to the bottom. Hove up the anchor by
the Ship as soon as possible and found his
body intangled in the Buoy-rope.*

The sun and wind are
hammer and tongs,
the deck our daily anvil.
Our hides are pickled,
tanned and calloused,
our sweat is brine,
our souls are leather.
The bark of the captain
is backed by the lash,
but more than that,
all of us fear the sea.

Peter Flower seaman fell from the main shrouds into the sea and before any assistance could be given him was drown'd, in his room we got a Portuguese.

We shake the vermin
out of our bread
and chew the ones
left in it. We sleep half-
smothered, hammocks
stacked. The cat is fairly
stuffed with rats, and still
they riddle every cask.
Some of the men
are like to rats.
We have our code.
But only a man
gone off his head
fears anything
more than the sea.

Wm Greenslade Marine, a raw young fellow, quiet and industrious, threw himself overboard and was not miss'd till much too late—driven by a trifling incident—incredible, the powerfull effects that shame can work upon young minds.

Some of us like
the stars in the black
the silent watch
the billow and snap
of filling sails.

Some of us live for
the grog and the rum
and the skirts in every port.
But all are wary
as long as we live
on planks above the sea,
for hardly a one
can swim a yard,
nor half a minute
keep from out
his panicked lungs
the softly murderous sea.

PARKINSON ON BOARD

A line to starboard, a shade to port—
braced, I sketch with the roll of the ship
tern, medusa, infant shark, whatever
net or shot can yield. Close cabin, ripe
with odor of dead specimens. But company
quite amiable: the learned botanist
Dr. Solander, most esteemed pupil
of great Linnaeus—portly, cheerful, modest.
Mr. Joseph Banks, vast in wealth and nearly
so vast in pride, and yet a genial nature,
not a moment's complaint in sickness
or harsh discomfort. A man of vigor,
scarce older than myself, prodigiously
curious, and said to be a shameless libertine.

They study, preserve, consult their books
and classify, delighting in each new species.
How wide the sea, how much is new!
Amazingly diversified are the works
of the Deity . . . the smallest object,
seen through the microscope, declares
its origin divine. I draw and listen.

RICHMOND AND DORLTON: NIGHT

Head to foot in musty hammocks
deep in the ship, in the fetid dark
two among dozens hanging
over the mess tables, a colony

of snoring, farting bats. The only
privacy is in the mind. These two
like all the rest imagined Tahiti—
rumored isle of easy life, abundant

food, warmth, voluptuous willing
women. Maybe they shared
in the seamen's bawdy talk by day:
girls half-bare, ripe and ready,

beauties all—some light brown,
others copper, some near white
as English girls, and the biggest tits
you ever laid a hand on. By night

perhaps they wondered—how willing
would the women be for them?
Civilized men, after all,
not savages. But black.

TIERRA DEL FUEGO

At anchor in the Bay of Good Success,
respite before they round Cape Horn
for the last five thousand miles to Tahiti.
Natives friendly enough, uninterested
in English tools, utensils, comforts, only
in ribbons and glass beads, though clothed
in meager scraps of seal or guanaco skin,
living on mussels in sieve-like huts
of sticks and grass—*as miserable
a set of People as are this day upon Earth.*

An exploring party, Banks in charge,
lost overnight on frigid slopes, whipped
by sleet and snow. Richmond and Dorlton
drank the party's liquor supply, lay down
in the snow and would not stir, though told
that farther down, men had managed
to make a small and smoky fire.

Entreaties failed. For worn and hungry men,
in the dark, on treacherous ground, to carry them—
impossible. (Was it? Buchan writhed in a seizure,
then lay stunned—Solander collapsed, exhausted—
yet both were saved.) Richmond and Dorlton
were covered with boughs and left,
a greyhound at their side. No record tells
if the dog was commanded to stay, or refused
to come away. Seamen sent at dawn would find
the servants dead, the dog reluctant to leave them.

How much thought, how much guilt,
did Richmond and Dorlton get from the others
that fitful night by the tremulous fire?

From Banks and Solander, Buchan the painter,
Monkhouse the surgeon, astronomer Green,
the servants and seamen who carried baggage?
No food but a vulture shot, cooked and split ten ways.
Nightlong turning their faces first to the fire, then
to snow-veiled wilderness, again to fire.

Richmond and Dorlton, blinking through twigs
at a sky spitting ice, might have had whole minutes
to dream. As senses ebbed, as viscous thought
slowed, gelled, stilled, did they step ashore
on the storied island, warm and free,
skin glowing in the kiss of the sun?

COOK: THE NATURE OF SEAMEN

The unvaried diet of a long sea voyage—
salt beef, salt pork, dry bread full of vermin
that *taste as strong as mustard*—if unrelieved
by fresh food allows scurvy *a footing
in the Ship*. This I proposed to prevent
by means of *Sour Krout, Portable Soup and Malt*—
a decoction of the latter given by the surgeon
to any man with the least symptom.

The Sour Krout the Men at first would not eate
and I made no attempt to compel them,
merely had it served to the officers daily,
letting the men *take as much as they pleased
or none atall*. In a week I had to ration it.

Such are the Tempers and disposissions of Seamen:
give them anything new, *altho it be ever
so much for their good,* they murmur, malign
the inventor, grumble, refuse; *but the Moment
they see their Superiors set a Value upon it,
it becomes the finest stuff in the World
and the inventor a damn'd honest Fellow.*

ONE LOOK BACK

ELIZABETH BATTS COOK

Mine the cottage
the pretty children
the beans and peas and turnips

mine the hollyhocks by the door
straight as soldiers
red as soldiers' coats

sturdy James, bright Nathaniel
like colts, like new
pennies

mine a letter eight months old
in eight months what may

I birth I tend I love

mine alone the bearing
Joseph who fought so hard
the hours hours Mrs. Wills no use
but to give me water

three fragile weeks the very air
brittle that September

tiny waxen face
a lace gown
a small grey stone

and my girl, my
Elizabeth! how dare he
gone three years saw her last her first
steps just taken could I not have hoped
the fever the tortured nights all mine—
I buried her, age four.

Hollyhocks
spring up again and bloom
again red the same
deep red. Come winter
the dried stalks will stoke the fire.

The
ENDEAVOUR
at Tahiti

APRIL–JULY 1769

REEF

all crevice and dart
life lurks
slips the pocked
branches of sea-forest
curves to brain coral's
round mound
scrabbles
into sand

glass-button eyes
flick of tails
veer of a corps de ballet

angelfish
in lemon or flame
lateral stripes (turquoise)
vertical (orange vanilla
black)

barracuda
a bullet
manta ray a sleek
storm cloud, sinister
undulation

floor level, lobster
in spiny armor
flounder and fire worm
urchin pincushion
star

improbable shapes
ingenious ways
to eat or not
get eaten

a world
impervious so far
to surface affairs

the view upward
just light, and a dazzle
of suspended particles

(most of them alive too)

FA‘A, AN OLD PRIEST

People crowding the shore stared and trembled.
Tutaha himself sent his heir into hiding
when the tall black shape appeared against

the lowering sun, poised at the mouth
of Matavai Bay. More than a year
since the Peretani departed, their visit

like a dream that shadows the day.
They left us iron tools, exotic creatures,
grief. They fed Purea's vain ambition.

Troublesome woman! Of noble family,
true—but not so noble as she presumed.
She made the foreign chief her *taio*, bond friend,

and though she wept a waterfall to see him go,
she thought herself invincible then. The more so
once her scheming lover, the priest Tupaia,

with sacred rites sewed the red Peretani cloth
to the high chief's red-feather girdle. With this
she plotted to invest her unworthy son. Now

the foreign chief and all his kin are bound
to avenge her defeat with their dreadful weapons.
Perhaps they know already Purea and Amo have fled,

their lands laid waste, warriors killed, Tupaia
gone over to the victors. Tutaha rules the district now.
But what is he against the guns?

FA‘A, AMBASSADOR

In such a crisis to whom could great
Tutaha turn? To me. I selected gifts
I knew would please the Peretani—
bananas, coconuts, vi-apples,
breadfruit, fish—and ordered stout men
to load the canoe and paddle.

Taio! Friend! I called (quite fearless)
as we approached. Strange faces
peered from above. And then
a face I remembered—and another—
and knowing me for a man of authority
they welcomed me aboard.

A different chief, tall and courteous,
presented me with a fine sharp hatchet.
I escorted him and his nobles ashore.
When they accepted the plantain boughs
of peace, the frightened people were vastly
relieved, and astonished. Are these Peretani

so weak, so unmanly, they dare not avenge
their *taio*'s defeat? Do they lack
all sense of honor? No. Rather,
the length and whiteness of my beard,
my dignity, my courage gave them pause.
Not that anyone has thanked me.

IMPRESSIONS OF THE NATIVES OF KING GEORGE'S ISLAND

Timorous, merry, facetious, hospitable,
generous with breadfruit, coconuts, hogs—
and *errant thieves*. Pickpockets quick as London's
(snuffbox? spyglass? gone). Let them on board,
they filch a bowl, a cleat, a knife—snatch

a midshipman's hat from his head—pry
the very glass from out the portholes. On land,
the astronomer's quadrant from a guarded tent.
The captain at rest (but not, he swears, asleep),
they stole his stockings from under his head.

Women so easy with favors, we could scarce
believe our luck, at first. Then the price
shot up *from a twenty or thirty penny nail*
to a forty penny, and some so Extravagant
as to demand a Seven or nine Inch Spike.

Nails by the sackful vanish from the hold, and none
knows a thing about it; men sleep on deck,
having spent their hammock nails. It's said
the *Dolphin* crept off creaking—so many cleats
and nails pried out she threatened to fall apart.

An indolent people. A long night's sleep,
and midday naps, and in that soft climate
the fruit drops into their mouths. And yet
they carve a sixty-foot canoe with an adze
and chisel made of stone, with human bones
for awls, with shark's teeth and shells.

They weep to see a sailor flogged, even
for crimes against themselves, and beg the captain

to let him go. And yet *inhuman custom*
among a certain lordly class—*enjoying
free liberty in love,* untroubled by consequence—
every infant *smother'd at the moment of birth.*

At times, to please their gods, they knock
a lowborn fellow on the head, truss
the corpse to a pole, and offer it in grisly
ritual. Their enemies' jawbones gleam
in the temple shadows. *The children
are remarkably kind to one another.*

PARKINSON: MORALITY

> *Most of our ship's company procured temporary wives amongst the natives . . . an indulgence which even many reputed virtuous Europeans allow themselves, in uncivilized parts of the world, with impunity; as if a change of place altered the moral turpitude of fornication: and what is a sin in Europe, is only a simple innocent gratification in America.*

So I wrote in my journal, and though the words
now burn me I will not strike them out.
Every common sailor beds a woman at any
opportunity, the ship's nails easy currency
for the old trade. Gentlemen and officers
much the same, though with slightly
more discretion, and finer currency, perhaps
a handkerchief or beads. Mr. Joseph Banks,
nightly with the beautiful Tiatia, by day
exudes the boldest satisfaction. In a week
virtue's standard fell to none but me—
"the Quaker," "Shyboots"—and Captain Cook.
Boys smirk and say at forty the captain
is too old. In truth, he is a faithful husband
whose unfeigned virtue alters not with change
of landfall. Of none other in the whole
ship's company could so much be said.

PARKINSON: DYE-MAKING

> The colour is good, but whether it will stand,
> I am unable to determine.
> —Sydney Parkinson, *Journal*

In a breadfruit grove a little inland
from the trafficked shore, in shade
of broad leaves she bent easy
as a willow, and the loose drape
of bark-cloth did not conceal
her perfect form. She picked

a leaf, and from a fig pressed out
upon it a milky fluid, rubbing gently.
I leaned close to see—warm scent
of coconut—slight scar at her clavicle,
tender pink edges—the mingled juices
of leaf and fig in an instant turned

crimson. My hand of its own will
touched her arm, fingers traced it
to her deft hand—the leaf fell—
I led her to a tent and there touched
everything alive in both of us, and all
the colors ever dreamed bloomed.

She left the carmine traces of her fingers
on my chest, my arms—truly marks of sin.
Although I never knew so sweet a sin,
nor one with rightness so suffused.

INCIDENT

Tafeha whispered a prayer to Hiro
who loves a bold thief—
the more audacious the act,
the better Hiro's shield—

then strolled up to the sentry
guarding the strangers' tent.
He knew the strangers' powers—
the ship that came and went

had blown canoes and men with clubs
to splintery bloody tatters.
Tafeha smiled. A keen
expectant crowd gathered.

A dance a jig a comic face—
the sentry stared and laughed—
Tafeha smiling shoved hard
snatched his musket and ran.

A boy, a midshipman
ordered *fire* men obeyed
with the greatest glee imaginable
two wounded *as if shooting
at wild ducks* running screaming
Tafeha shot dead

Cook came running, his orders
*check the petulance of the Sailors
restrain the wanton use of Fire Arms*
and Banks *if we quarrelled
with those Indians we should not
agree with angels* hasty

efforts to reassure, to justify
the death yet make amends.
A few—then more—returned—
fearful—calling them "friends."

Soon the British and islanders laid
the plantain boughs of peace,
drank coconut milk together,
talked and laughed at ease.

What was one man's reckless death?
Theft was a capital crime.
And the chief could cow his rivals
if British guns were on his side.

The captain had a ship to provision—
ninety mouths to feed—
the transit of Venus to measure,
the empire's advance to lead.

And yet that night *we retird to the ship
not well pleased—guilty
no doubt of the death of a man
the severest laws of equity*

would not have condemnd.
The widow laid cloths at her feet,
slashed her face with a shark's
tooth, stabbed, shrieked.

Then, stone silent, a stone's
calm in her ribboned face,
she gathered the bloody cloths
and flung them in the bay.

Ebb of day made silhouettes
of palm and plantain, till night
absorbed them. On the black bay
delicate wavelets, light

as blind men's curious fingers,
felt along the elmwood keel
and lightly broke
against the white-oak hull.

AND EVERYWHERE THERE WAS JOSEPH BANKS

who dashed after the stolen quadrant—sole means
of measuring the transit of Venus—with only
one man to back him, seven sweaty miles in-country
away from ship marines guns where anything
could have happened and marched back
victorious

who advised Cook when Buchan the painter died
*I sincerely regret him as an ingenious and good
young man* to bury him at sea for fear of violating
sacred customs unknown *but his loss to me is
irretrevable, my airy dreams of entertaining
my freinds in England with the scenes here are
vanishd*

who ebullient confident handsome made friends
of the men and lovers of the women, rudely
ignoring the chief's wife *ugly enough in conscience*
to ply with gifts *a very pretty girl with a
fire in her eyes*

whose elaborate dress, assurance, sparks of arrogance
marked him for islanders a true aristocrat
for they were every bit as class-ridden
as the English

who observing the transit of Venus invited islanders
to look through the telescope and tried to explain
in Tahitian

who was curious enough to lift the cloth on a corpse
already dropping to peices with putrefaction observe
within all parts of his flesh an abundance of maggots
and identify the species

who arrived a botanist and departed a meticulous
ethnographer—learned language, described clothes
food houses tools tattooing cloth-making dyeing
fishing canoe-building navigating—ate roast dog
(delicious), got his arm tattooed, tested the protocols
of sexual hospitality

who wrote the first-ever account of surfing—men diving
with infinite ease in breakers so *dreadfull no European
could possibly have saved his life* and stood with Cook
*admiring this very wonderfull scene
for full half an hour*

who having asked permission of the chief stripped
to a loincloth blackened his face and ran with a funeral
party—the Chief Mourner wielding his club tipped with
shark's teeth, *the people everywhere fly before the Heiva
as sheep before the wolf*—and after, dipped
in the cool river with the rest to scrub the soot
off one another

who the first day on the island strolled with gentlemen
and officers *followed by the whole train* of natives
through *groves of Cocoa nut and bread fruit
trees loaded with a profusion of fruit and giving
the most gratefull shade* beneficent handing out
beads and trinkets

and that night exuberant in the journal
declared this green island *an arcadia
of which we were going to be
kings*

THE SAILORS PREPARE TO DEPART

Haul out provisions, examine the lot,
the beef and the suet, the raisins and malt,
the flour and peas and pork.
Haul every barrel back into the hold,
half-spoiled to the front for the earliest use.

Hare in the underbrush, hawk in the sky,
seaman upon the sea.

With lines to the masts, careen the ship
over to starboard, then over to port,
her hundred-foot length to be scraped and paid
with brimstone and pitch to the waterline,
in the blaze of the pitiless sun.

Trout in the river, whale in the deep,
seaman upon the sea.

Carpenters carve new stocks for the anchors,
the old eaten up by the worm.
Sixty-five casks to be filled with water
and ferried from river to ship.
Dismantle the fort and chop it for firewood.
Stow the sticks on board.

Hare to earth and hawk to nest,
trout to crevice, whale adrift.
In a wooden ship, by work and wit
he comes, if his luck and the weather permit,
the seaman home from the sea.

COOK: DEPARTURE

Every man lies aboard tonight. Still in the dark,
I listen to every creak of the ship, the rhythmic
rush of breakers, every birdcall, every
snore from the gentlemen's cabins.

This much accomplished: timed the passage
of Venus across the sun, charted the island
for future landings, recorded language
and customs, collected plants and animals.
Recovered two deserters, Gibson and Webb—
prey to the charms of girls and an easy life.
Two dozen lashes each are due, once underway.

In various soils Mr. Banks has planted
seeds from Rio de Janeiro: lemon, orange,
watermelon, lime. We leave a quantity
of tools. And how many curious minds
have we stirred, with our telescopes,
our foreign language, Mr. Parkinson's art,
our blunt disapproval of barbarous customs?

Yet I cannot persuade myself we have bettered
their lot. One man dead, and venereal
distemper rife, though *I did all in my power
to prevent its progress*—with the assistance
of precisely no one. It will plague the entire
South Seas, *to the eternal reproach
of those who first brought it among them.*

At any rate, we move. Of the natives
who offered to join us, I received Tupaia,
a most intelligent man, to guide and mediate
as we explore the islands. Then, south
and farther, colder south to discover or disprove
once and for all the fabled continent.

TUPAIA LEAVING

Not since red-haired Tafa'i, grandson of the moon,
wandered in his sacred canoe, pulling new islands
out of the sea—

not since Hiro the trickster, god of thieves,
journeyed to distant islands, stole from the birds
the rare red feathers to make the ancient
high chief's girdle—

not since Tafa'i traveled to the land of the dead and back
has any man made such a voyage.

I will guide this ship among the islands, knowing
by currents, by stars and constellations,
the true direction,

praying to Tane for fair winds, finding deep channels
through the reefs. Upon each shore performing
the ceremonies of peace.

Then, beyond all the islands I know.
Far and farther, beyond our language, beyond
even the cries of the birds, their small sharp voices
lost in the sky.

So Tafa'i must have traveled, farther than we ever dreamed,
to make the island of these strange men.

Farewell, Tahiti, where I rose and fell with the tides
of rival chiefs, where I leave no wife, no child, no kin.
I have friends among these foreigners, and bring Taiato,
now full ten years old, chosen to learn my priestcraft.

Child of the sun—a smiling nature, bright music always
from his flute. Child too of the stars, quick to learn
what the stars and I can teach.

Why then should tears threaten as the ship begins to glide,
the canoes fall back, distance folds the trees into the mountains?
I stand a long time waving.

And now no looking back—except
to remember with each sunrise my home on Ra'iatea,
the vicious invaders, years of exile.
If I survive,

as Hiro returned with treasure, I will return with guns
and with all my kin take back our land, destroy
our enemies, string up their jawbones.

COUNTERPOINT

C. 1770

I never beheld statelier men.
A superb race, handsome and well built.
Women so well proportioned.
Few faces have I seen which have more expression in them.

IN THE PORTS, 1800S

Slovenly, haggard and diseased.
Scarcely anything so striking or pitiable
as their aimless, nerveless mode of spending life.

TRUTH IS THE DAUGHTER OF TIME
—Francis Bacon

But which? Time has a bevy of daughters—
they all say their name is Truth. Perhaps
it's that one—aloof, mature, setting aside
her book to observe. Or the one painting canvas
with brilliant oils, the fortune teller, the one
herding yaks, or planting rice, or twirling
a shiny baton in the Christmas parade. Or that one,
wild-eyed, babbling to herself in a corner.

Truth is the daughter of time, it's time
for a daughter. Or is it truth that mothers?
Surely a daughter's the truth of time.
Look for her where you stand. Sift the earth,
the glittery sand, the waves that spill and thin on the beach
only to slip away.

IN MATAVAI BAY

In Matavai Bay
each anchor's slow
fall to the sea floor a
depth charge that roiled
the bay, rocked
the land

After the first,
ships came at odd
intervals, then more and more
often: emissaries of empire,
commerce,
god

Whaling ships
coasted in, folding
their great wings to settle
for a bit, eat well for a change,
screw women, stock up,
move on

Bountiful,
stern, the white-sailed
sugar daddies gave, for sex
and hogs and breadfruit: old shirts,
dysentery, hatchets, beads,
nails, smallpox, rum

Missionaries
met ridicule, met rage;
some fled, others in stone
certainty persisted, held sway,
calling the *timorodee* dance
shameful,

the gods false
and impotent, solemn
sacrifice barbarity, rum wrong—
depth of ritual, all color, exuberance
given up for hymns and dour
prohibitions

It took time
to forget how to make
a stone adze, beat bark into
cloth; time to learn to love rum,
to learn (the first strangers
gone)

they'd been given
syphilis; time—one or two
brief generations—for a people
to be decimated; time to know
they were just
flotsam

their island
wrecked on its own
reef, splintered by percussive
ripples from each
anchor's slow
fall

INCIDENTAL

They wanted food, water, sex.
They meant to advance science, seek adventure,
serve the king, win souls for Christ, or earn a wage
and stay alive. It was purely incidental

that the fleas on the rats on a French ship carried plague

that surgeons declared men clean, allowed them ashore,
      not knowing venereal disease could incubate
      months without symptoms

that the introduction of alcohol made alcoholics

that girls gave birth to half-European babies to be
      brought up with love, or killed

that sheep a world away from their rock-walled pastures
      left behind as gifts suffered unsheared
      till they died of the heat

that cats—another gift—ate flightless birds
      to extinction

that islanders came to despise alike infanticide and tattoo artistry,
      human sacrifice and the phenomenal skill
      of canoe-builders and cloth-makers

It was incidental
that decent men intending no harm fixed Tahiti
      in the crosshairs of longitude and latitude
      for every predatory ship to come

that within thirty or forty years the population declined 90 percent

that no woman started, inflicted or exacerbated any of this

Incidental
that people who had known where they stood
       on their island like a great fish
         in a family in a class in the bright world
         above the ancestors and gods

now perched idle shrunken backward on a volcanic dot
       in the Pacific and did not know

Alone
as in the beginning the one god Ta'aroa
       stood alone in the void and called and called
       but nothing replied

Being a god he changed himself into the universe

They were not gods, and Tetumu the rock of foundation
       had cracked

Though the dome of the sky still soared
       where Tane had propped it on pillars of stars
       they could no longer hold up their heads beneath it

POSSESSION

Dolphin's red pennant
on a spar thrust into sand
King George's Island

French carved in an oak plank
La Nouvelle Cythère

tall Spanish cross
La Isla de Amat

a few native kings
with guns and missionaries
the last queen
forced into a French
protectorate

entitling German cruisers
to shell it (why not) in '14

now *la plus grande île
de Polynésie Française:*

118 islands including
the Tuamotus where
three decades
181 nuclear explosions
a quarter above ground
diffused as far as
New Zealand and Peru

Tahiti by far
the most visited
Welcome to paradise!

where fierce peaks and perfectly
clear azure turquoise aqua

regarding no name
are themselves
are beautiful
are

THE CHIEF MOURNER

The body laid on its bier, a kinsman dons
the costume, swells with its power.

A necklace, tangled braids of sennit,
for Tane, god of peace and beauty.

At the shoulders, five gleaming pearl shells:
Hina, the moon goddess.

Iridescent shell fragments stitched into rows:
the eyes of dead chiefs transformed into stars.

An apron, polished bits of coconut shell,
evokes a tale of escape from the underworld.

Most sacred of all, the mask: a fanned crown
of red-tipped feathers (a rainbow) above

a divided face, half black for the spirit world,
half shining white shell (the bright world

from which the dead depart) and in it
one small hole for the right eye.

He is the Chief Mourner,
lord at once of rule and misrule

who leads loud followers
blackened with candlenut soot

who mourns with rage, awakens the gods,
wields a club armed with shark's teeth

before whom the terrified people
scatter and flee

who, the ritual ended, must put away
the sacred costume, having traced

the knife-border of the spirit world,
and emerge, spent, seeing with both eyes

how dark are the veins that lace
the broad bright leaf

of the world he thought he knew.

COUNTERPOINT

They may be said to have had
no history, not before the Europeans,
because time was not a line
but a still pool, a womb
in which they floated, time
without change. Come rain or sun,
streams flowed in the highlands,
fish swam to their nets, something
edible was always in season.
Coconuts, breadfruit, tropic
apples swelled and dropped.

No history, for wars were brief, killed
few, changed little. No history,
for the social hierarchy stood firm—
gaps between strata are small where all
have food in plenty, and no one has much else.
So little to steal, and the world so warm,
their houses had no walls. No history

They were in the throes of history—
their own—when Europeans
split *before* from *after*.
'Oro, two-minded god of fertility
and war, crushed the ancient
peaceful cult of Tane. Often now
the terrible drums, the stranger clubbed dead,
trussed, eye and hair plucked for ritual.
As the season of scarcity began
lords of ceremony declaimed a cold
farewell to the gods.

Factions, chieftains, stoning clubbing stabbing
island to island, women pinned, wombs hacked out.
Between wars aristocrats preserved
their studied pallor in the shade.
Neither prison nor whippings. A thief
caught in the act tied to large stones
and dropped in the sea.

in that timeless island but yours mine his hers—the real story—of each hard birth, first steps on the coral skirt of the sea, tattooed initiation, the making of children. Unhurried days, gathering fruit, pounding and dyeing bark into cloth, with stone tools carving canoes from felled trees, three times a day bathing in the river. Until at last one went into night, laid on a scaffold for birds to eat, and the bones dropped to the black volcanic sand. So, and so, by sun, by moon.

Time ruled from the instant of each hard birth. Did it sift slowly, that time by the rhythmic sea, measured by the dull rhythms of beating bark-cloth, carving wood? Or rush from child-words and child-songs through dawn of sex, marriage, childbirth and work and battle, ceremony to ceremony? Till the body was laid out in honor or chopped for trophies or left in the bloody communion of massacre, for the jumbled bones to whiten by sun, by moon.

Then the ships brought history, and the sailors brushed it like dust from their clothes, and even the captains who'd planned *to treat them with all imaginable humanity* spoke human history in every word, and in the tropic air it smoked and lingered like insidious ash of a thousand distant fires, and settled in their lungs.

The sailors took their story back and set it free. In the best drawing rooms all talk was Arcadia, the noble savage, the titillating island of love. In sewage-laced slums the half-starved, overworked, hopeless, diseased wondered. And the radical dream of a place where nobody, not one soul, was poor took root.

AFTERWORD

James Cook and the *Endeavour* went on from Tahiti to New Zealand, where he mapped both islands, proving for the first time that they were not part of the mythical Southern Continent. The expedition continued up the east coast of New Holland (Australia), where the *Endeavour* was seriously damaged on the Great Barrier Reef and came extremely close to destruction and the loss of all on board, not to mention a vast collection of plant and animal specimens; hundreds of illustrations by Parkinson, Tupaia, and others; and the journals that give us so much insight into these early encounters.

Remarkably few lives were lost on this three-year voyage until the *Endeavour* reached Batavia (Jakarta), where the men were struck with malaria and dysentery. In Batavia or soon after departure for the final six months' journey home, thirty of the ship's people died, including surgeon William Monkhouse, astronomer Charles Green, and **Sydney Parkinson**, who left behind 280 finished paintings and about a thousand drawings as well as a vivid and thoughtful journal, which unfortunately survives only in the version edited by his unstable brother.

Tupaia and his acolyte, Taiato, also died at this time. Taiato was a sweet, charming boy, much liked by the Englishmen, but Tupaia was unpopular because of his sense of superiority to all but Cook, Banks, and a few others. (Cook: "a Shrewd Sensible, Ingenious Man, but proud and obstinate.") Yet Tupaia had played a vital role as navigator, translator, and cultural intermediary as the *Endeavour* traveled among the Pacific islands, sparing the expedition much hardship, confusion, and violence.

Cook visited Tahiti twice more over the next eight years, during his second and third voyages to the Pacific. His journals include perceptive comments about the troubling impact of Europeans on the people of Tahiti and other Polynesian islands as well as about his own frustrations in dealing with them. He was killed by natives in Hawaii in 1779.

Elizabeth Batts Cook died in 1835 at the age of ninety-three, having outlived her husband and all six of her children, the last of whom died when she had forty-one years yet to live.

Joseph Banks returned to England to widespread celebrity. He intended to sail on Cook's second Pacific voyage as well, but withdrew, enraged, when the navy would not modify the ship to accommodate all his extensive retinue. Other than one natural-history exploration of Iceland, he remained mostly in England, but he continued to be deeply involved in science. For forty-two years he was the powerful and autocratic president of the Royal Society, England's premier scientific organization, and worked to improve and disseminate economically useful plants and to encourage scientific collaboration across national boundaries. He also played a role in the plan to send convicts to colonize Australia. Though sometimes arrogant and high-handed, he was a man of lively curiosity, kind, and deeply loyal to his friends. Cook named the Banks Peninsula on New Zealand's South Island for him, and William Bligh named Banks Island in Vanuatu in the Pacific. An island in Canada's Northwest Territories also carries his name.

Daniel Solander returned to England to resume his work in the natural history collections of the British Museum and to prepare a manuscript on the flora of New Zealand. He continued to collaborate with Banks, and they were close friends, traveling together to Iceland, the Hebrides, and Wales. He died of a stroke at Banks's home at age forty-nine. His name survives in his invention called the Solander box, still used to store prints and herbarium specimens; in Solander Gardens in London, Point Solander at Botany Bay in Australia, and the Solander Islands off New Zealand; and in the names of many plant species.

George Robertson continued his naval career after the *Dolphin* returned to England. As a lieutenant he fought the American rebels, chasing and seizing ships up and down the coast from New Jersey to Florida and into the Caribbean. He retired in his late forties.

Finally, at least one more individual deserves a few words:

THE CELEBRATED GOAT

> She sailed around the world with Wallis and again
> with Cook and never in all the years went dry—
> confined for months on hard, heaving, grassless

ground, her food stale if not rotten, daily
milked for the officers' tea. Ah, but now
her lords have made amends: at Banks' request
the famous Dr. Johnson pens a Latin couplet
in her honor. By this, engraved on the silver collar
she wears for her remaining pastured years
she is rewarded, raised above her peers.

ACKNOWLEDGMENTS

This book and I owe an enormous debt to my husband, Paul Cody, who while writing his own books constantly encouraged me, with more faith in this project than I could sometimes muster myself. Thanks also to Martha Collins, poet and friend, whose work I admire, who has taught me so much, and whose lively spirit and literary ferocity always inspire me.

I am also grateful to the eminent scholar Anne Salmond, whose writings opened up Tahitian life and points of view for me, and to the incredibly comprehensive Cornell University Library.

NOTES

Throughout this book, I have tried to be as true to the historical record as possible. Where I invent or speculate, I use questions and tentative words like "perhaps." I have not presented anything as fact that I know to be false.

At the same time, in the interests of poetry, I did not want to be rigid. Representing the cross-cultural encounters and the otherness that Tahitians and Europeans perceived in each other, I sometimes found it useful to include an observation by the *Dolphin*'s men in the *Endeavour* section and vice versa. I have also occasionally taken small liberties with quotations, such as omitting an insignificant word for better rhythm, or correcting a misleading spelling error, and I have not always used ellipses where something is omitted.

"Prophecy"
Vaita's prophecy is recorded in Salmond, *Aphrodite's Island*.

"George Robertson's Poem"
The entire poem, except the phrases in parentheses, is taken from the journal of George Robertson, master of the *Dolphin*.

"Approach"
Uneven as a piece of crumpled paper . . . highest peaks: Parkinson journal.

"*Marae*"
Jawbones: Salmond, *Aphrodite's Island*.

"Purea, a 'Great Woman'"
The *Dolphin*'s men called Purea "queen of Tahiti," though her sphere of influence was only part of the island. She and her allies were defeated by rivals in a bloody battle that took place between the visits of the *Dolphin* and the *Endeavour*.

Aute: hibiscus.

"Skin"
Quotes chiefly from the journals of Joseph Banks and George Robertson.

"Tupaia, High Priest"
Ra'iatea: Pronounced, approximately, Rah-ee-ah-TAY-ah.
Peretani: Tahitian pronunciation of Britain/British.

"Points of Interest"
Whiteness: Prince of Nassau, quoted in Salmond, *Aphrodite's Island*.
No other Gods: Philibert Commerson, quoted in Salmond, *Aphrodite's Island*.

"James Douglas, 14th Earl of Morton"
Excerpts from the "Hints" manuscript, which was probably written in response to accounts of the *Dolphin* at Tahiti, are quoted in Salmond, *Aphrodite's Island*.

"The Mission"
Every blockhead: Edward Smith, *Life of Sir Joseph Banks* (1911), 15–16, apparently quoting a letter from Banks.

"James Cook, Captain"
From a prentice boy: Cook, *Resolution* journal.
A man who has not: Cook, *Resolution* journal.

"Joseph Banks, Botanist and Patron"
A great Inattention . . . Love of Play: letter of Edward Young, assistant master at Eton, to Joseph Banks's father, quoted in Patrick O'Brian, *Joseph Banks: A Life*.
Richly enamelled: Everard Home, describing the epiphany that led Banks to a consuming interest in nature, quoted in O'Brian, *Joseph Banks: A Life*.

"Daniel Solander, Botanist"
Such good philosophers: Solander, quoted in Edward Duyker, *Nature's Argonaut: Daniel Solander, 1733–1782*.
A masterpiece: Carolus Linnaeus, quoted in Carol Kaesuk Yoon, *Naming Nature: The Clash between Instinct and Science*.

"Sydney Parkinson, Artist"
I went on board: Parkinson journal.

"Sailors"
In heaving the Anchor: Cook, *Endeavour* journal, Sept. 14, 1768, at Madeira; the first death of the voyage.

Peter Flower: Cook, *Endeavour* journal, Dec. 2, 1768, at Rio de Janeiro. The phrase "from the main shrouds into the sea" is from Parkinson's journal, substituted for Cook's "over board."

Wm Greenslade . . . fellow: Cook, *Endeavour* journal, March 26, 1769.

Quiet . . . young minds: Banks journal, March 25, 1769.

"Parkinson on Board"

Amazingly diversified: Parkinson journal.

"Tierra del Fuego"

As miserable a set of People: Cook, *Endeavour* journal.

"Cook: The Nature of Seamen"

Taste as strong as mustard: Banks journal.

A footing in the Ship . . . honest Fellow: Cook, *Endeavour* journal.

"Fa'a, Ambassador"

Fa'a played an important role in dealings with the British, but the men of the *Endeavour* found him comically pompous.

"Impressions of the Natives of King George's Island"

Timorous, merry . . . thieves: Parkinson journal.

From a twenty or thirty penny nail . . . Spike: Robertson journal.

An indolent people . . . into their mouths: Parkinson journal.

Inhuman custom: Cook, *Endeavour* journal.

Enjoying free liberty: Banks journal.

Smother'd: Cook, *Endeavour* journal.

Remarkably kind: Parkinson journal.

"Incident"

Tafeha: The thief's name was not recorded; I have given him a Tahitian name.

A boy, a midshipman . . . wild ducks: Parkinson journal.

Check the petulance . . . Fire Arms: Earl of Morton, "Hints" delivered to Cook and Banks before the *Endeavour* voyage.

If we quarreled: Banks, quoted in Parkinson journal.

We retird . . . condemnd: Banks journal.

"And Everywhere There Was Joseph Banks"

All quotations from Banks's journal.

"Cook: Departure"
All quotations from Cook, *Endeavour* journal.

"Counterpoint" part title page

I never beheld: Parkinson journal.

A superb race: Prince of Nassau (who traveled with Bougainville), quoted in Salmond, *Aphrodite's Island.*

Women: Robertson journal.

Few faces: Banks journal.

Slovenly: Frederick Debell Bennett, *Narrative of a Whaling Voyage Round the Globe, from the Year 1833 to 1836.*

Scarcely anything: Daniel Wheeler, 1834, quoted in Moorehead, *The Fatal Impact.*

"Counterpoint"

To treat them with all imaginable humanity: Cook's orders to his men upon arrival in Tahiti (*Endeavour* journal).

Afterword

Samuel Johnson: *Perpetua ambitâ bis terrâ praemia lactis / Haec habet altrici Capra secunda Jovis.* Translated by R. W. Chapman: "After a double circumnavigation of the globe, the goat, second [only] to the goat that nursed Jove, has this reward of her milk that never failed."

SELECTED SOURCES

Baker, Simon. *The Ship: Retracing Captain Cook's Endeavour Voyage.* 2003.
Banks, Joseph. *The Endeavour Journal of Sir Joseph Banks.* Ed. J. C. Beaglehole. 1962.
Beaglehole, J. C. *The Life of Captain James Cook.* 1974.
Cook, James. *The Journals.* Selected and edited by Philip Edwards. 2000.
Druett, Joan. *Tupaia: Captain Cook's Polynesian Navigator.* 2011.
Duyker, Edward. *Nature's Argonaut: Daniel Solander, 1733–1782.* 1998.
Fara, Patricia. *Sex, Botany & Empire: The Story of Carl Linnaeus and Joseph Banks.* 2003.
Gerzina, Gretchen. *Black London: Life before Emancipation.* 1995.
Holmes, Richard. *The Age of Wonder: How the Romantic Generation Discovered the Beauty and Terror of Science.* 2008.
Howarth, David. *Tahiti: A Paradise Lost.* 1984.
Lamb, Jonathan, Vanessa Smith, and Nicholas Thomas, eds. *Exploration and Exchange: A South Seas Anthology, 1680–1900.* 2000.
Moorehead, Alan. *The Fatal Impact: The Invasion of the South Pacific, 1767–1840.* 1966; expanded edition, 1987.
O'Brian, Patrick. *Joseph Banks: A Life.* 1987.
Parkinson, Sydney. *A Journal of a Voyage to the South Seas, in His Majesty's Ship the Endeavour.* 1773.
Robertson, George. *The Discovery of Tahiti: A Journal of the Second Voyage of H.M.S. Dolphin Round the World.* Ed. Hugh Carrington. 1948.
Salmond, Anne. *Aphrodite's Island: The European Discovery of Tahiti.* 2010.
———. *The Trial of the Cannibal Dog: The Remarkable Story of Captain Cook's Encounters in the South Seas.* 2003.
Yoon, Carol Kaesuk. *Naming Nature: The Clash between Instinct and Science.* 2009.

http://agroforestry.net/projects/traditional-tree-initiative. Excerpts from *Traditional Trees of Pacific Islands*, ed. Craig R. Elevitch. 2006.